Careers in the
US Army

Michael V. Uschan

ReferencePoint
Press®

For more information, contact:
ReferencePoint Press, Inc.
PO Box 27779
San Diego, CA 92198
www.ReferencePointPress.com

LIBRARY OF CONGRESS CATALOGING-IN-PUBLICATION DATA

Uschan, Michael V., 1948–
    Careers in the US Army / by Michael V. Uschan.
        pages cm. -- (Military careers)
    Includes bibliographical references and index.
        ISBN 978-1-60152-934-3 (hardback) -- ISBN 1-60152-934-1 (hardback) 1. United States. Army--Vocational guidance. 2. Soldiers--United States. I. Title.
        UB323.U84   2016
        355.0023'73--dc23
                                                                                    2015034203

Contents

A Wide Variety of Careers

The US Army is the oldest and largest branch of the military. It was created at the start of the American Revolution in 1775 and in 2015 celebrated its 240th birthday. The image of a soldier carrying a rifle into battle in the historic conflict with England that led to creation of the United States is as true today at it was then. The army's primary mission, then as now, is to serve as the nation's main offensive force on land.

Many Career Choices

The army today offers a wide variety of career choices, some intended for entry-level personnel who receive all their training from the army and others requiring advanced skills in medical care, computer technology, and construction. The army has ten career categories—administrative support, intelligence and combat support, arts and media, legal and law enforcement, combat, mechanics, computers and technology, medical and emergency, construction and engineering, and transportation and aviation. The army offers more than 150 different jobs, including many that people might not expect to see, such as army band musicians, foreign language interpreters, chaplains, and deep-sea divers.

Each army job is known as a military occupational specialty, and each category has a number of available jobs. For example, in addition to maintaining and running the army's vast computer system, soldiers in computers and technology install cable systems for computers and other media and use various technologies to intercept and analyze enemy data and transmissions. And construction and engineering soldiers include carpenters, masons, and plumbers, as well as several types of engineers. The army needs mechanics to maintain and fix motor vehicles, helicopters, and even missile systems. And although most army activities are land based, job opportunities exist on water and in the air, from cargo handlers to divers to helicopter pilots.

With so many choices, deciding on a career path in the army might seem overwhelming. The Armed Services Vocational Aptitude Battery (ASVAB) is a multiple-choice test that determines attributes recruits have that qualify them to perform certain jobs. It tests a variety of skills and knowledge in ten areas, including mathematics, science, mechanics, and electronics. Some military occupational specialty positions require candidates to attain a certain score in a particular area of the test to qualify for that job.

Women in the Army

Many jobs in the army are open to both men and women. In fact, the number of women in the army has steadily risen over the last three decades. In 1983 women made up 9.8 percent of the total army, which includes active duty, US Army Reserve, and Army National Guard soldiers. By 2014 that number had risen to 16.3 percent. One reason for the increase is that the army has opened more jobs to women, including many that directly support combat operations. This change has sometimes placed women in combat situations despite the prohibition against female combatants. Army sergeant Rebekah Havrilla served in Afghanistan from September 2006 to September 2007 as an explosive ordnance disposal technician. In an interview with a military publication, Havrilla admitted that while deactivating or destroying enemy explosives, "I saw combat repeatedly [and] I was in a couple of firefights."

The ban on female combatants was being reviewed by the army and other branches of the military. Women have traditionally been barred from the infantry, for instance, because of fears they were not physically or emotionally strong enough for combat. But in 2013 the US secretary of defense stated that all army positions would be opened to women by January 1, 2016, unless military authorities showed why this change should not take place.

US Armed Forces: Pay

In the US Armed Forces, pay for both enlisted personnel and officers depends on rank and years of service. Promotions depend on performance in addition to number of years served, with higher ranks translating to higher pay grades. The two graphs show monthly salaries commonly reached in the first four years of service.

Enlisted Pay

Monthly Salary Ranges for Enlisted Personnel with 0–4 Years in Service

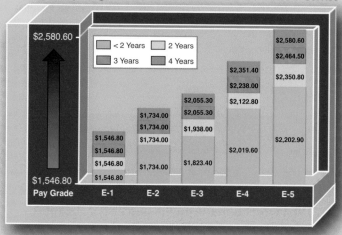

Officer Pay

Monthly Salary Ranges for Officers with 0–4 Years in Service

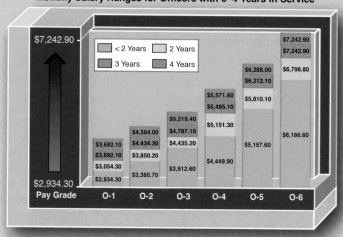

Note: Monthly salary ranges in both graphs are based on enlisted and officer pay scales effective January 1, 2015. The pay scales described here do not take into account the value of health benefits or housing and other allowances.

Source: Defense Finance and Accounting Service, "Military Pay Charts, 1949 to 2015," December 23, 2014. www.dfas.mil/militarymembers/payentitlements/military-pay-charts.html.

Enlisted and Officer Ranks

Members of the active duty army are full-time soldiers. Those in the army reserve and National Guard are part-time soldiers who can be called to active duty to handle domestic emergencies or fight in foreign countries. All branches of the army include enlisted soldiers and officers, two main categories based on military rank. Most soldiers begin their military career as privates, the lowest army rank, and advance through several levels of enlisted rank, including corporal and sergeant. The lowest-ranked officer is a lieutenant, followed by captain, major, colonel, and general. As soldiers rise in rank, they are gradually given authority to command more and more soldiers. A corporal, for example, would be in charge of several soldiers, whereas officers would command progressively larger groups.

Enlisted soldiers can become officers if they become eligible for and complete Officer Candidate School. An example is John Shalikashvili, who in 1952 at age sixteen immigrated to the United States with his family from Poland. He was drafted into the army in 1958 as a private after graduating from Bradley University. He went through Officer Candidate School to become a lieutenant, eventually became a general, and ended his career as chair of the Joint Chiefs of Staff.

Training for Technical Jobs

More army jobs today than ever before require advanced technical skills and college degrees. The Reserve Officers' Training Corps program helps college students pay for their education while also training to be officers when they graduate. The army also offers scholarships in special fields like medicine and dentistry for people who enlist after graduation. In addition, soldiers in the reserve and National Guard can receive financial aid to pay off student loans they acquired before joining the army or to pay for education while serving in those part-time branches of the army.

Soldiers who leave the army are also eligible for educational benefits to prepare them for civilian jobs. Milwaukee native John Ocasio joined the army in 1987 as an infantryman. A paratrooper who learned to parachute out of airplanes, Ocasio received medical care several times after breaking small bones in jumps. In an interview Ocasio said, "I remember being at the clinic and seeing these guys one day with these little X-ray machines and I thought, 'Oh man, that would be a cushy job.'" Ocasio returned home to his native Milwaukee when he retired after twenty years in the military, and he went to school to become a radiation therapist, a high-paying medical job. His education was funded by the Montgomery GI Bill, which has helped veterans pay for college or other training since it was enacted at the end of World War II. Many soldiers stay in the army until they retire. Soldiers who retire after twenty or more years receive a pension based on a percentage of their basic monthly pay, which everyone of the same rank receives, while those leaving after 40 years receive 100 percent of their basic pay at the time they retire.

The many benefits soldiers receive from employment in the army make it a good choice as a workplace. Additionally, soldiers are rewarded by the sense of serving their country.

Infantryman

What Does a Member of the Infantry Do?

Infantryman is an entry-level military occupational specialty for enlisted personnel. This position is the basic unit of the army's main land combat force. Although the primary mission of infantrymen is to fight and defeat enemy soldiers, they also perform many other tasks. Other duties include maintaining and storing vehicles and weapons used in combat; performing reconnaissance missions to gather information about enemy troop movements; capturing, guarding, and transporting enemy soldiers to secure areas; and patrolling areas the army controls to safeguard civilians from enemy soldiers. During peacetime, soldiers engage in drills, take classes, and prepare themselves physically and mentally for future combat; they also perform humanitarian missions or assist with disaster relief.

There are twenty-five infantry jobs associated with combat, some of which require advanced training or education such as firing heavy artillery, rockets, portable cannons called mortars, and missiles. Other combat positions include driving and fighting in tanks, locating and neutralizing mines, and operating two-way radios and signal equipment to relay and receive

At a Glance:

Infantryman

Minimum Educational Requirements
High school diploma or GED; minimum score of 90 on the combat portion of the ASVAB

Personal Qualities
Able to deal with extreme stress; good physical condition; work well with a team

Working Conditions
All different environments; primitive and harsh in combat situations

Salary Range
Monthly salary depends on pay grade and years of service

Future Job Outlook
Good through 2022

battle orders. Cavalry scouts are considered the "eyes and ears" of the army. They precede other soldiers into enemy territory on foot or in vehicles to locate enemy positions, calculate enemy strength, and provide other vital information for battle. In a video on goarmy.com, Private First Class Aaron Alley of Sterling, Michigan, explains that by providing such information, he protects fellow soldiers from surprise attacks: "[I] take care of my men." Alley also takes great pride in his work: "For a 21-year old guy I have a pretty darn important job. Three years ago I was just getting out of high school. You learn a lot of responsibility, you get paid, and you help to serve your country. Not too many can do this job."

How Do You Become a Member of the Infantry?

Education

Some high schools offer Junior Reserve Officers' Training Corps programs. Students interested in the military learn lessons and skills that will help them succeed in an army career. Anyone interested in the infantry should participate in sports and fitness programs because the infantry demands high levels of physical strength and stamina. Martial arts instruction would also prepare people for combat situations.

Infantrymen go through fourteen weeks of basic combat training and advanced individual training in their specialties, which is usually conducted at Fort Benning in Columbus, Georgia. Training takes place in both the classroom and the field. Training includes how to operate and maintain weapons and vehicles used in combat. Infantry soldiers use small arms, which include rifles and other guns. Infantrymen also learn how to read maps and use them to navigate through unfamiliar areas and how to operate army communications equipment. They are also taught how to prepare fighting positions, like where and how to dig trenches to protect them from enemy fire and how to erect fences and other barriers to limit movement of enemy soldiers and secure areas they are defending. Specialized training for some soldiers includes learning to parachute from airplanes into combat and how to operate mortars, small portable cannons that can fire explosive shells as far as 4 miles (6.4 km).

Skills and Personality

An infantryman is the core combat soldier in all the branches of the US military. In addition to developing fighting skills during training, infantrymen need to be physically and psychologically strong to handle the rigors of combat. Like all soldiers, infantrymen must be willing to obey all orders from their superior officers, including orders given during combat that might expose soldiers to enemy fire or other dangers. Soldiers must also be able to work as part of a team because they fight as a unit, not as individuals. Individual soldiers must not only work together to defeat an enemy force but to protect each other during combat. In basic combat training, all soldiers learn seven core values that the army expects them to follow. The seven values are loyalty, duty, respect, selfless service, honor, integrity, and personal courage. Courage in battle does not mean soldiers are free of fear; it means that soldiers will do what their training has taught them despite their fears. Infantrymen, like all other soldiers, are expected to adhere to those seven values in their daily lives even when they are not on duty.

On the Job

Working Conditions

During combat, living conditions on the front line can be primitive and harsh. Soldiers often sleep and live in tents and temporary housing that lack indoor plumbing and provide little relief from heat, cold, rain, or snow. When on the move, they live in the open. Soldiers must carry weapons, food, and other supplies and equipment that can weigh 60 pounds (27 kg) or more. In a secure base, soldiers eat meals prepared by cooks, but in the field they only have MREs—meals ready to eat. MREs are self-contained, individual field rations that have been freeze-dried and dehydrated. One MRE contains a full meal, including a main course such as beef teriyaki or meatloaf, powdered beverages like coffee that are mixed with water, and dessert. A chemical in the packet activated by exposure to water heats the meals.

11

A US Army infantryman guards the perimeter while others search a village near the Afghanistan-Pakistan border. The infantry is the basic unit of the army's main land combat force.

Combat in a war zone is hard physically and mentally. The threat of attack is constant whether infantrymen are on base or in the field. Soldiers in combat have to deal with their own fear of being wounded or killed as well as seeing it happen to other soldiers or civilians. Combat is a brutal experience that can horrify soldiers. Former army lieutenant Sean Parnell wrote *Outlaw Platoon* about combat in Afghanistan. In an interview about his book in 2012 for an army publication, Parnell claimed no one is ever the same after experiencing war: "Combat veterans come back forever changed. The innocence and distance that you once knew in the United States is burned away forever in your first experience in combat." The incident that changed Parnell happened in February 2006 shortly after he had arrived at an army base that was under attack in eastern Afghanistan. The base included civilians as well as soldiers. When a young girl was wounded, Parnell carried the bleeding girl to an aid station to save her life. Instead, she died in his arms. Her death made Parnell realize how terrible war could be and continues to haunt his memories.

Infantrymen do not fight as individuals but as members of military units. The smallest army unit, the squad, consists of eight to sixteen soldiers and is usually led by a sergeant. A platoon consists of three to four squads and is led by a lieutenant or other officer and a sergeant. The platoon is the basic unit capable of operating in combat by itself. Platoons are also part of other military units such as a company (three to four platoons) and a battalion (three to five companies).

Despite having different skills, soldiers in combat situations work together and depend on each other to defeat the enemy. They also try to keep each other safe during battle. John Ocasio experienced combat in Panama in 1989 and the First Gulf War in 1991. In an interview with the author, Ocasio explained how soldiers depend on each other: "You have to be able to learn to be a team player. That's because you realize you have to have your buddy's back in combat. And all the other guys are also protecting you. Nobody else is going to look out for you except your buddies. And if you don't have your buddy's back something bad can happen either to him or yourself." He also said that sharing such dangers creates a strong emotional bond between soldiers: "What I liked most about the Army was the guys you met; you get so close to each other that it becomes like a brotherhood. That was great."

Earnings

The basic pay active duty soldiers receive is based on their rank and length of service. New recruits enter the army as privates, the army's lowest rank. The basic pay for privates is $18,378.00 annually. That base salary goes up steadily, based on rank and length of service. For example, a private first class, the next-highest rank, earns $21,664.80, and that salary increases further every two years he or she serves. Officers earn more than enlisted soldiers, ranging from $34,862.40 for a lieutenant to $52,869.60 for a major.

Salary, however, is just one part of military compensation. Soldiers and their families receive medical and dental care at little or no cost through a military health care plan. Soldiers are also eligible for low-cost group life insurance. Soldiers who live on military bases receive free housing and meals. Soldiers who live off a military base receive an allowance to cover housing and meals. Soldiers also receive allowances for military clothing and official travel. In 2014 the average active duty soldier received a total compensation package of benefits and pay worth $99,000.

Soldiers in combat zones receive $225 per month in hostile fire and imminent danger pay. A variety of salary bonuses is also available for active duty soldiers who serve in foreign countries where the cost of living is high or for reenlisting when their tour of duty is done. Depending on how long they serve, soldiers are also eligible for compensation for schooling when they leave the army. Soldiers get thirty days of vacation annually. Depending on what their missions and training dictate, soldiers are off on weekends and national holidays and get sick days as needed.

Opportunities for Advancement

Infantry soldiers can rise in enlisted rank. They can also become officers by attending Officer Candidate School; an enlisted soldier who becomes an officer is known as a "mustang." Infantrymen can boost their careers by attending specialized schools to learn advanced skills for other jobs. At the Defense Language Institute, for example, soldiers learn to read and write foreign languages—a valuable asset in foreign countries. Another specialized school is the Pathfinder School, where students learn how to navigate through unknown terrain and establish safe landing zones for other soldiers.

What Is the Future Outlook for the Infantry?

In 2016 the army reduced the number of soldiers on active duty in the regular army to 475,000, due to the withdrawal of soldiers from wars in Iraq and Afghanistan. However, it still had 547,007 soldiers in its reserve forces—349,881 in the National Guard and 197,126 in the army reserve. Despite the slight reduction in active duty soldiers, job opportunities for qualified individuals in the army are expected to remain good through 2022, due to continuing military and terrorist threats to the nation's security in various parts of the world.

Since the end of the draft in 1973, the military has met its personnel requirements with volunteers. The army needs to fill entry-level and professional positions as members move up through the ranks, leave the service, or retire. Thus, despite the army drawdown, its recruiting goal for 2016 is 66,500 because of retirements and people leaving the service.

What Are Employment Prospects in the Civilian World?

When infantrymen leave the military, they take with them many valuable work habits and skills that can help them find civilian jobs. The military teaches soldiers self-discipline and the importance of teamwork, as well as how to closely follow orders and take pride in what they do. All of these are valuable traits that can help make them good employees in almost any job. Upon leaving the service, soldiers can receive financial aid for higher education to prepare them for civilian jobs.

Human Intelligence Collector

At a Glance:

Human Intelligence Collector

Minimum Educational Requirements

High school diploma or GED; minimum score of 101 on the language section of the ASVAB

Personal Qualities

Fluency in or aptitude for languages; good people skills; strong written and verbal communication skills; resourceful; analytical

Certification and Licensing

Secret security clearance

Working Conditions

In an office or in the field

Salary Range

Monthly salary depends on pay grade and years of service

Future Job Outlook

Good through 2022

A human intelligence collector is an entry-level military occupational specialty for enlisted personnel. Human intelligence, sometimes referred to as HUMINT, refers to facts and data gathered through contact with people. Human intelligence collectors gather information so soldiers in combat can more efficiently fight and protect themselves from enemy attacks. Human intelligence encompasses facts about the strengths and weakness of enemy soldiers, information on what the enemy is planning to do, and details about possible battle sites. Duties include questioning civilians or captured soldiers, reviewing enemy documents, taking part in missions to acquire human intelligence, and analyzing and preparing reports about information that is collected. In a goarmy.com forum, a soldier who identifies herself as Rae 12 explains the essential nature of the job: "Think of [it] as collecting puzzle pieces. In the end you want to know what the whole picture is, sometimes you'll be interviewing and when needed you'll be putting the information together. In the end it's your job to find the details the army needs to put the puzzle together."

Human intelligence collector is one of thirty-three different jobs in the army career field of intelligence and combat support. In addition to gathering and analyzing information from a variety of sources, soldiers in this career area perform other tasks to support combat operations. Ammunition specialists store and issue all types of ammunition from bullets to guided missiles, and divers perform underwater missions involving reconnaissance, demolition, and salvage operations. Human intelligence collectors, though, work most closely with other military intelligence workers such as cryptologic linguists, who monitor and translate into English information they get from enemy signals and documents. Psychological operations specialists are enlisted personnel who use information collectors gather to create various media products to influence people in foreign combat zones to accept and act favorably toward US troops. Most battles are waged with guns and explosive devices, but enemy forces can use high-tech weapons that most people are unfamiliar with. The chemical, biological, and nuclear specialist is educated about such weapons and trained to protect military and civilian populations if they are used.

How Do You Become a Human Intelligence Collector?

Education

Students can prepare for this army career by taking classes in psychology, computer science, and foreign languages. Junior Reserve Officers' Training Corps programs would also prepare students for military life. Collectors must have a high school diploma or GED and a minimum score of 101 on the language section of the ASVAB. They must also be able to qualify for a secret security clearance, which means their past will be investigated for criminal or possibly anti-American activities.

All members of the army must first go through ten weeks of basic combat training. Human intelligence collectors then receive twenty weeks of advanced individual training in their specialty. A big part of advanced individual training for this position is learning how to talk to people and extract information that will help the army defeat the enemy in battle. Staff Sergeant Thomas Applebee, an instructor in this course, says in an article in a military journal that human intelligence collectors "take a lot of pride in the fact that ours is the oldest intelligence discipline there is." Military intelligence is collected today in many high-tech ways, including images from drones or satellites orbiting earth. But Applebee says questioning people is still one of the best methods to acquire intelligence. He claims the simplicity of this method is the key to its effectiveness: "We don't need a computer screen. I need a pen, a piece of paper, and someone to talk to, to do my job. [We've] been doing this for hundreds of years, and we can keep doing it." Collectors also learn to analyze information from interviews and prepare reports, maps, and charts based on data they collect so they can share that information with other soldiers who need it to do their job.

Skills and Personality

Human intelligence collectors have to be comfortable talking with all kinds of people, including strangers, because that is the most important way they gather information. Knowing how to speak a foreign language is a plus but not a requirement to become a collector. Even if the language a new recruit speaks is not one the collector would use while in the army, it shows that the candidate has the ability to learn a foreign language. Because captured soldiers and other people may lie when asked questions, collectors need to be good judges of character so they can determine if the person is telling the truth. In a video on the army's official home page, Sergeant Magdalena James says training helps collectors know if someone is lying: "The army taught me how to talk to people, to gain intelligence from what they're saying and what they're not saying." Collectors sometimes work in combat zones, so they must be willing to face the possibility of being attacked. Computer skills are also a must for human intelligence collectors so they can analyze data and prepare and distribute reports. Human intelligence collectors handle information classified as secret. Because of that, candidates have to obtain security clearance, which means the army will investigate their past in detail to make sure they are fit to do such a job.

On the Job

Working Conditions

The most basic duty of human intelligence collectors is to gather information by talking to people on the ground. Sometimes these conversations take place in secure military camp settings. Other times human intelligence collectors are required to work in surrounding villages or other areas outside the camp, which means they can encounter dangerous situations, including being attacked by enemy soldiers in combat situations. Carolyn Schapper, a member of the Virginia Army National Guard, worked as a collector in both Iraq and Afghanistan. In an interview with the Public Broadcasting System, Schapper admitted she often questioned civilians in areas that contained armed enemies. Schapper said, "I was armed. I would go out almost every day, and I would go into the villages and the cities, and get out of my truck, and walk into their homes [and talk to people]." Collectors talked to civilians to find out things like what they knew about enemy troop movements or the level of animosity against US troops in the area. Collectors sometimes talked to people just once. But they might interview people many times who were in positions of authority or who had contacts with the enemy and were willing to share that information.

Some interviews are conducted with subjects friendly to US forces. However, collectors sometimes have to question hostile subjects, including captured terrorists, enemy soldiers, and civilians. One of the problems in extracting information from such subjects is that they may lie when answering questions. Staff Sergeant Jonathan Bobo, a military intelligence instructor, explains in a story for a military newspaper that this forces collectors to assess the way subjects answer questions to determine if they are telling the truth: "You have to be able to read someone else and you won't get that by being shy or looking away. You have to look at everything from their body language to their expressions." Learning how to do that is something that takes time and practice and is one of the most important skills collectors need to do their job.

Earnings

The basic pay active duty soldiers receive is based on their rank and length of service. New recruits enter the army as privates, the army's lowest rank. The basic pay for privates is $18,378.00 annually. That base salary goes up steadily, based on rank and length of service. For example, a private first class, the next-highest rank, earns $21,664.80, and that salary increases further every two years he or she serves. Officers earn more than enlisted soldiers, ranging from $34,862.40 for a lieutenant to $52,869.60 for a major.

Salary, however, is just one part of military compensation. Soldiers and their families receive medical and dental care at little or no cost through a military health care plan. Soldiers are also eligible for low-cost group life insurance. Soldiers who live on a military base receive military housing and meals for free. Soldiers who live off a military base receive an allowance to cover their housing and meals. Soldiers also receive allowances for military clothing and official travel. In 2014 the average active duty soldier received a total compensation package of benefits and pay worth $99,000.

Soldiers in combat zones receive $225 per month in hostile fire and imminent danger pay. A variety of salary bonuses is also available for active duty soldiers who serve in foreign countries where the cost of living is high and for reenlisting when their tour of duty is done. Depending on how long they serve, soldiers are also eligible for compensation for a college education when they leave the army. Soldiers get thirty days of vacation annually. Depending on what their missions and training dictate, soldiers are off on weekends and national holidays and get sick days as needed.

Opportunities for Advancement

Human intelligence collectors are highly valued in the army because their job is vital to successful combat operations and to the safety of fellow soldiers. Collectors who are skilled at performing those tasks will gradually be given more authority and more important assignments. And as they become proficient at their job, they will rise in rank so they can guide the efforts of other collectors. Although the human intelligence collector position is for enlisted personnel, highly talented soldiers in this field may be able to become officers by going to Officer Candidate School.

What Is the Future Outlook for Human Intelligence Collectors?

In 2016 the army reduced the number of soldiers on active duty in the regular army to 475,000, due to the withdrawal of soldiers from wars in Iraq and Afghanistan. However, it still had 547,007 soldiers in its reserve forces—349,881 in the National Guard and 197,126 in the army reserve. Despite the slight reduction in active duty soldiers, job opportunities for qualified individuals in the army are expected to remain good through 2022, due to continuing military and terrorist threats to the nation's security in various parts of the world.

Since the end of the draft in 1973, the military has met its personnel requirements with volunteers. The army needs to fill entry-level and professional positions as members move up through the ranks, leave the service, or retire. Thus, despite the army drawdown, its recruiting goal for 2016 is 66,500 because of retirements and people leaving the service.

What Are Employment Prospects in the Civilian World?

The skills and work habits human intelligence collectors develop and refine in the army would be a plus for people in jobs involving research or business planning. They could also help former soldiers gain employment in government agencies such as the CIA or NSA, both of which are in the business of collecting human intelligence. Language skills and the knowledge soldiers gain about culture and traditions in foreign countries in which they work could also prove valuable to civilian employers. Service in the armed forces can also be a plus when applying for any job because many employers like to reward soldiers for their military service by hiring them.

Health Care Specialist

Health care specialist is an entry-level military occupational specialty for enlisted personnel. Specialists are part of the large group of doctors, dentists, nurses, and other medical personnel who provide health care for soldiers and their families. The main duties of health care specialists include providing emergency medical treatment, some primary care, promoting good health and illness prevention, and evacuating sick, wounded, or injured soldiers to hospitals where they can receive more advanced medical care. On a military base, specialists perform a variety of medical tasks, including preparing patients for surgery and making sure doctors have the equipment and supplies they need for surgery. They help provide outpatient and inpatient care and treatment for soldiers and their families and perform medical procedures such as preparing blood samples for laboratory analysis.

During times of war, specialists serve as combat medics who

At a Glance:
Health Care Specialist

Minimum Educational Requirements
High school diploma or GED; minimum score of 101 on the general technical portion of the ASVAB

Personal Qualities
Good with people; empathetic; able to think and work under stressful conditions; detail oriented

Working Conditions
In a hospital setting or in the field, including combat situations

Salary Range
Monthly salary depends on pay grade and years of service

Future Job Outlook
Good through 2022

provide emergency medical treatment for soldiers wounded in battle. Most platoons, which can vary in size up to more than sixty soldiers, have a medic. The main duty of medics in combat is to do whatever they can to keep wounded or injured soldiers alive and prepare them for evacuation to medical centers that can provide more advanced medical treatment.

Specialists are part of a vast group of medical professionals that compose the Army Medical Corps. This vast array of army health care workers provides a complete range of health care for both soldiers and their families. Medical personnel include many different types of doctors, surgeons, psychologists, and even obstetricians to handle pregnancies. The position of health care specialist is for enlisted soldiers; personnel with more advanced medical training and expertise, like doctors, have officer rank. However, health care specialists are vital to health care because they perform a wide variety of tasks to assist doctors and other medical professionals. The job of an army health care specialist is often compared to that of an emergency medical technician in civilian life. But in an army video, Staff Sergeant Fabiola Surena explains, "We are so much more than that in the military—[we] work in trauma hospitals, primary care clinics, ob-gyn (obstetrics and gynecology), you name it, we're very versatile. We get a whole lot of skills that put us at a level between a nurse and a doctor." That versatility is a necessity. Health care specialists work in the relative safety of military bases, where doctors and other medical personnel are available to help them treat patients. But they may also function as medics in combat zones, where their lives may be at risk. In those situations, the overall knowledge and skill they have will be the only thing capable of saving the lives of other soldiers who become sick or are wounded.

How Do You Become a Health Care Specialist?

Education

High school students who have an interest in becoming a health care specialist should take classes in biology and chemistry and, if available, a medical pathway program. Courses in first aid, CPR, and the

As part of a readiness training exercise in Vietnam, a US Army health care specialist takes a patient's vital signs. During the exercise, citizens of the host nation receive free medical care, and medical personnel have a chance to improve their skills.

use of automated external defibrillators that are offered by the Red Cross or other agencies are also good preparation.

Training for this military occupational specialty begins with ten weeks of basic combat training, followed by sixteen weeks of advanced individual training. That training teaches health care specialists how to care for patients in both a hospital setting and in the field, as well as emergency medical techniques such as applying tourniquets to stop bleeding and applying plaster casts to protect broken limbs. Health care specialists assist doctors in surgery, so they also learn how to sterilize surgical equipment. Private Nour Arodak, who learned to be a health care specialist, admits in an *Army Times* story that "the training is pretty challenging." His training included a twelve-day field exercise on a base near San Antonio, Texas, that tested all the skills he had learned. What made the exercise even harder was that it took place during extremely hot weather, and instructors pushed the future health care specialists to the limit of their endurance to simulate real-life conditions as combat medics.

Skills and Personality

One of the most important personality traits a health care specialist must have is the desire to help other people, a trait that made Sergeant Tracey Lyons a good fit for this position. In a video on the goarmy .com website, Lyons explains that for her, "the cool part about my job is the reward I get from taking care of Soldiers." That attitude is vital because health care specialists sometimes have to place the safety of their patients above their own, even in combat situations in which their own lives are in danger.

Specialists also must be able to handle stressful situations and think quickly in emergencies. An example of how combat medics have to act instantly in a crisis to save lives occurred in 2012 in Afghanistan when Devon Jackson treated Staff Sergeant Christopher Walker. Walker received multiple severe injuries when a bomb exploded and threw him 50 feet (15 m) through the air. Walker was trying to defuse a roadside improvised explosive device (IED) when another explosive went off. Jackson rushed to Walker and began applying tourniquets to various wounds so Walker would not bleed to death. In a *USA Today* newspaper story, Jackson said he was shocked at the injuries and did not know how many tourniquets he used on Walker: "I just remember I was putting on tourniquets." The actual total was seven. But Jackson's ability to perform his job instantly in a moment of crisis and horror was the reason Walker survived the explosion.

On the Job

Working Conditions

Health care specialists spend most of their time on military bases in clinics and hospitals, where they help provide medical care for fellow soldiers and their families. They perform a wide variety of jobs, from taking a patient's blood pressure to assisting in trauma centers to save the lives of people injured in military or civilian accidents.

Although that type of work can be difficult psychologically if patients die, the job of a health care specialist becomes much harder during times of war.

Combat medics are sometimes nicknamed "Doc" by other soldiers, due to their medical skills. However, they function as regular members of platoons in the field or in combat situations until they need to care for wounded or injured soldiers. They carry the same gear as other soldiers but are often armed only with a handgun instead of a rifle because fighting is not their primary responsibility during combat. Medics also have to carry a backpack loaded with bandages, tourniquets to stop bleeding, drugs to alleviate pain, and other medical supplies.

In combat, whether in the field or at a more secure military base, their job is to provide emergency care to preserve the lives of wounded or injured soldiers and prepare them for evacuation to a hospital. It is important to provide such care as quickly and efficiently as possible so the wounded soldier can be transported to a facility that can provide a higher level of care. In an Army Strong video, Staff Sergeant Eric Zlatkin says speed is even more important during combat because of the danger both the wounded soldier and health care specialist face from enemy combatants: "If you're taking fire you don't want to stick around for too long so you just do the basics." In the video Zlatkin explains that tourniquets are the medic's most important piece of equipment because it is necessary to stop wounds from bleeding too much or the soldier will die.

Earnings

The basic pay active duty soldiers receive is based on their rank and length of service. New recruits enter the army as privates, the army's lowest rank. The basic pay for privates is $18,378.00 annually. That base salary goes up steadily, based on rank and length of service. For example, a private first class, the next-highest rank, earns $21,664.80, and that salary increases further every two years he or she serves. Officers earn more than enlisted soldiers, ranging from $34,862.40 for a lieutenant to $52,869.60 for a major.

Salary, however, is just one part of military compensation. Soldiers and their families receive medical and dental care at little or no cost through a military health care plan. Soldiers are also eligible for low-cost group life insurance. Soldiers who live on a military base receive military housing and meals for free. Soldiers who live off a military base receive an allowance to cover their housing and meals. Soldiers also receive allowances for military clothing and official travel. In 2014 the average active duty soldier received a total compensation package of benefits and pay worth $99,000.

Soldiers in combat zones receive $225 per month in hostile fire and imminent danger pay. A variety of salary bonuses is also available for active duty soldiers who serve in foreign countries where the cost of living is high and for reenlisting when their tour of duty is done. Depending on how long they serve, soldiers are also eligible for compensation for a college education when they leave the army. Soldiers get thirty days of vacation annually. Depending on what their missions and training dictate, soldiers are off on weekends and national holidays and get sick days as needed.

Opportunities for Advancement

Soldiers who do well in this position have the opportunity to rise in rank as in any other type of army job. The army also provides opportunities for education that could help experienced or talented health care specialists learn to do other jobs in the Medical Corps that require more advanced training or education.

What Is the Future Outlook for Health Care Specialists?

In 2016 the army reduced the number of soldiers on active duty in the regular army to 475,000, due to the withdrawal of soldiers from wars in Iraq and Afghanistan. However, it still had 547,007 soldiers in its reserve forces—349,881 in the National Guard and 197,126 in the army reserve. Despite the slight reduction in active duty soldiers, job opportunities for qualified individuals in the army are expected to remain good through 2022, due to continuing military and terrorist threats to the nation's security in various parts of the world.

Since the end of the draft in 1973, the military has met its personnel requirements with volunteers. The army needs to fill entry-level and professional positions as members move up through the ranks, leave the service, or retire. Thus, despite the army drawdown, its recruiting goal for 2016 is 66,500 because of retirements and people leaving the service.

What Are Employment Prospects in the Civilian World?

The training health care specialists receive prepares them for a variety of civilian jobs in the medical field, such as emergency medical technician, paramedic, physical therapist, nurse, or doctor. Some of these civilian jobs require additional training or education. After leaving the army, most veterans are eligible for educational benefits under the Montgomery GI Bill, a program that has helped former soldiers pay for higher education since World War II.

Combat Engineer

Combat engineer is an entry-level military occupational specialty for enlisted personnel. This position was opened to women in 2015. Combat engineers provide two main types of assistance during combat—mobility and countermobility. Combat engineers improve troop mobility by making it easier for their fellow soldiers to move across rough terrain or geographic obstacles. For example, they build fixed or floating bridges across rivers and other bodies of water. Sometimes they also have to clear enemy explosives from roads, fields, and other areas over which troops will travel. *Countermobility* is a military term that involves constructing obstacles such as barbed wire or fences or destroying infrastructure to make it harder for enemy soldiers to attack. Sometimes combat engineers blow up bridges or roads to hamper the enemy's mobility. Or they might place land mines and explosives to make it dangerous for the enemy to attack or move freely. The job of combat engineers is to enhance both mobility and countermobility to help fellow soldiers do their jobs and survive. In an Army Strong story, this is how Sergeant First Class Jeremy Cruz sums up his work as a combat engineer: "My

At a Glance:
Combat Engineer

Minimum Educational Requirements
High school diploma or GED; minimum score of 87 on the combat portion of the ASVAB

Personal Qualities
Able to focus on details and big picture; interested in how things fit together; meticulous; strength and stamina

Working Conditions
In the field, including combat situations

Salary Range
Monthly salary depends on pay grade and years of service

Future Job Outlook
Good through 2022

job is to create and destroy obstacles on the battlefield and to conduct route clearance" for fellow soldiers.

Combat engineers are part of the army's construction and engineering units. Soldiers in construction and engineering include trained engineers who draw up plans for bridges, buildings, and other structures, as well as skilled workers such as carpenters, masons, plumbers, and electricians who build them. Other jobs in this job group include water-treatment specialists who purify and store water; soldiers who build airfields, roads, and dams; and others who are trained in repairing construction equipment from bulldozers to electric generators. Some members of these units also use heavy machinery to move tons of earth or other material in various construction projects.

How Do You Become a Combat Engineer?

Education

To prepare for this military occupational specialty, high school students should take industrial arts classes, if available, to develop a working knowledge of tools and machinery. Preengineering or other engineering-type classes would also be valuable. And participation in Junior Reserve Officers' Training Corps programs helps student become familiar with military life.

Combat engineer recruits go through fourteen weeks of training, including basic combat training and advanced individual training at the US Army Engineer School at Fort Leonard Wood, Missouri. Training occurs in the classroom and the field. During training, combat engineers learn a wide variety of skills, many of which involve dealing with explosives. Demolition classes teach combat engineers how to use explosives to clear physical obstacles that hinder troop movement. There are also classes on how to find and deactivate or safely detonate explosives planted by the enemy. Combat engineers also learn how to construct wire obstacles and operate heavy equipment such as the heavily armored Assault Breacher Vehicle, which resembles a tank and is used to clear explosives from roads.

"Sapper" is a military nickname for combat engineers. An advanced level of training in combat engineering is offered in the Sapper Leader Course. It is open to combat engineers and other enlisted soldiers, male or female, with a rank of specialist or higher and officers with the rank of at least captain. The twenty-eight-day course at Fort Leonard Wood concentrates on teaching students tactics and leadership skills so they can lead small units into battle. The course teaches demolitions, medical care, and how to travel and conduct combat operations on land, in water, and in mountainous areas. Students also learn how to organize patrols, perform reconnaissance, and ambush enemy soldiers. Graduates earn the right to wear a Sapper Tab, one of four army tabs that show a soldier has specialized individual skills. The tab is a small, arched red patch that says "SAPPER" and is placed on the shoulder of the soldier's uniform.

Skills and Personality

It is helpful if combat engineers have basic mechanical and construction skills and know how to use hammers, saws, and other simple tools to build things. Candidates should also have an interest in basic engineering principles and how to use them to accomplish various tasks. The desire to enhance such skills and knowledge is also necessary. Combat engineers should also have a confident attitude that they can accomplish any task no matter what problems they encounter, because they will encounter a wide variety of problems in their job. Combat engineers also work extensively with explosives, which can be dangerous. To ensure their safety and that of other soldiers, while working with any explosive device they must be able to concentrate on every detail of the job at hand.

On the Job

Working Conditions

Combat engineers who work in active war zones work under extremely dangerous conditions. During the recent US wars in Afghanistan and Iraq, for instance, combat engineers were responsible for finding and eliminating IEDs. IEDs are often hidden along paths or roads that US troops travel. These deadly devices explode from the pressure of someone walking on them or a vehicle driving over them.

During explosives training, US Army combat engineers tie a time fuse to a detonating-cord firing system. Explosives are a primary tool used by combat engineers, whose job is to enhance mobility and countermobility for their fellow soldiers.

Combat engineers use electronic equipment—or in some cases dogs that can smell explosive material—to find IEDs. One of the things that makes this job so dangerous is the very real risk of some devices exploding while combat engineers are searching for them. And, as with any soldier in a war zone, enemy fire is also a constant threat. In some instances, to prevent destruction of IEDs, enemies have attacked combat engineers as they searched for the explosive devices. In 2013 Corporal Antonio Burnside was killed by enemy fire while trying to clear IEDs from a highway in Afghanistan. As a result of many such incidents, the army began dispatching armed soldiers to guard the combat engineers while they hunted IEDs. In a story on the army's home page, Sergeant First Class Bryan Butler says Burnside's death was not in vain and that his death "probably saved many lives because we changed our tactics."

Combat engineers also use explosives to help vehicles and soldiers move through difficult terrain in a task called route clearance. Engineers can blast roads through hills and other geographical obstacles hindering movement by using C4, a military explosive. Corporal Carlo Heres says that learning to handle explosives correctly and safely is one of the most important parts of his job. In a story for a military publication, Heres says, "This is the bread and butter as a combat engineer." He declares, "There is no problem you can't solve [with] the proper amount of explosives. That is something we believe in. That is something we preach."

The duties of combat engineers, however, are not confined to blowing things up, even though that is a big part of their job. Their mission also includes building things, from laying floating bridges across water so vehicles can travel over them to building highways and various types of structures. Combat engineers in Iraq and Afghanistan repaired highways damaged by explosives, renovated buildings so they could be used by US forces, and rebuilt airfields. They also built structures at entry points into cities and around other key areas that made it easier for soldiers to keep them secure from hostile forces.

Earnings

The basic pay active duty soldiers receive is based on their rank and length of service. New recruits enter the army as privates, the army's lowest rank. The basic pay for privates is $18,378.00 annually. That base salary goes up steadily, based on rank and length of service. For example, a private first class, the next-highest rank, earns $21,664.80, and that salary increases further every two years he or she serves. Officers earn more than enlisted soldiers, ranging from $34,862.40 for a lieutenant to $52,869.60 for a major.

Salary, however, is just one part of military compensation. Soldiers and their families receive medical and dental care at little or no cost through a military health care plan. Soldiers are also eligible for low-cost group life insurance. Soldiers who live on a military base receive military housing and meals for free. Soldiers who live off a military base receive an allowance to cover their housing and meals. Soldiers also receive allowances for military clothing and official travel. In 2014 the average active duty soldier received a total compensation package of benefits and pay worth $99,000.

Soldiers in combat zones receive $225 per month in hostile fire and imminent danger pay. A variety of salary bonuses is also available for active duty soldiers who serve in foreign countries where the cost of living is high and for reenlisting when their tour of duty is done. Depending on how long they serve, soldiers are also eligible for compensation for a college education when they leave the army. Soldiers get thirty days of vacation annually. Depending on what their missions and training dictate, soldiers are off on weekends and national holidays and get sick days as needed.

Opportunities for Advancement

As in any army position, soldiers are able to rise in rank as they gain more expertise and experience. Combat engineers can also take the Sapper Leader Course to learn new skills that will make them elite combat engineers.

What Is the Future Outlook for Combat Engineers?

In 2016 the army reduced the number of soldiers on active duty in the regular army to 475,000, due to the withdrawal of soldiers from wars in Iraq and Afghanistan. However, it still had 547,007 soldiers in its reserve forces—349,881 in the National Guard and 197,126 in the army reserve. Despite the slight reduction in active duty soldiers, job opportunities for qualified individuals in the army are expected to remain good through 2022, due to continuing military and terrorist threats to the nation's security in various parts of the world.

Since the end of the draft in 1973, the military has met its personnel requirements with volunteers. The army needs to fill entry-level and professional positions as members move up through the ranks, leave the service, or retire. Thus, despite the army drawdown, its recruiting goal for 2016 is 66,500 because of retirements and people leaving the service.

What Are Employment Prospects in the Civilian World?

The construction and mechanical skills combat engineers learn will prepare them for a variety of jobs in the construction industry, including positions that involve building demolition and inspection. And being in the army will help veterans get such jobs for two reasons: Employers like to reward veterans for their service to the country, and employers appreciate the discipline, willingness to work hard, and other on-the-job traits the military instills in soldiers. Also enhancing their postmilitary careers is the fact that veterans are able to get financial support for higher education to get a good job. And the experience combat engineers have can especially prepare them to go to school to become engineers or train for other construction jobs, including masons, carpenters, and electricians.

Watercraft Operator

Watercraft operator is an entry-level military occupational specialty for enlisted personnel. The army is the US military's largest land fighting force. However, to support soldiers based on land, especially during combat, the army maintains a fleet of boats. The army's fleet of more than one hundred boats is used to transport personnel, equipment, and vehicles to army bases around the world and sometimes to participate in humanitarian missions. In addition to being charged with navigation and operation of these boats, army watercraft operators load, unload, and deliver cargo. Watercraft operators must also learn how to defend their boats against enemy attacks.

The rapid, secure movement of troops and supplies is vital to success in combat. Although the army is primarily a land-based fighting force, at times it needs to transport personnel and supplies on rivers, lakes, and oceans. Thus, boats are part of the army's overall system of transportation. That system naturally depends most heavily on trucks

At a Glance:
Watercraft Operator

Minimum Educational Requirements

High school diploma or GED; minimum score of 99 on the mechanical maintenance portion of the ASVAB

Personal Qualities

Comfortable being at sea for long periods of time; able to work independently and as part of a team; good sense of direction

Certification and Licensing

Required every five years in all specialties

Working Conditions

On boats of various sizes doing a variety of jobs

Salary Range

Monthly salary depends on pay grade and years of service

Future Job Outlook

Good through 2022

and other wheeled vehicles to move supplies on land. The army transportation system also includes cargo specialists, who oversee delivery of supplies worldwide via ships and trains, as well as mechanics and other technicians to keep a wide variety of vehicles operating on both land and sea.

Watercraft operators fulfill the army's vital transportation needs on water by piloting and navigating boats to move cargo. Watercraft operators perform many jobs, including maintaining and running engines that propel the boat, navigating the boat to its destination, loading and unloading cargo, and defending the ship and those aboard when attacked. One of the important jobs is standing watch, a nautical term for a wide variety of types of oversight of the boat and the boat's mission. Personnel who stand watch for specific periods are constantly looking for anything that can endanger the boat, its crew, or its mission; how the ship's engines and other mechanical parts are performing; and to make sure the ship stays on course. The watch includes using radar and sea charts to make sure the ship stays clear of reefs or areas too shallow for it to pass through.

Watercraft operators also use boats to land troops and supplies on shore to fight the enemy. The most famous example of this occurred on June 6, 1944, when boats carried an estimated 156,000 US, English, and Canadian soldiers to the beaches of Normandy on the coast of France during the invasion known as D-Day. The complicated landing paved the way for the Allied victory in World War II. Watercraft operators communicate with other vessels in combined military operations electronically. They can also communicate by placing flags on their ships that correspond to an international letter code and spell out messages people on other ships can interpret.

How Do You Become a Watercraft Operator?

Education

Students interested in a career as a watercraft operator can prepare themselves by learning how to sail and operate boats or by acquiring other nautical skills like navigating using compasses and maps. Enrolling in a Junior Reserve Officers' Training Corps program where available would also prepare students for military life. Job training for a watercraft operator requires ten weeks of basic combat training and six weeks of advanced individual training with on-the-job instruction. Army watercraft operators learn how to do a wide variety of jobs. Because most army boats are smaller and have fewer crew members than the much larger ships found in other branches of the military, crew members often have multiple responsibilities. This means that they sometimes have to help each other to perform various tasks. Training takes place in the classroom as well as aboard boats like the ones on which new recruits will serve. The extensive sea-based training they receive includes information on types of army boats, how to handle boats in various sea and weather conditions, and basic navigation techniques. One of the workhorse army boats is the Landing Craft Utility 2000, which is 174 feet (53 m) long and can transport soldiers and even large cargo items like tanks. Watercraft operators learn how to land boats on beaches and other types of shoreline. They also have to learn how to safely maneuver and pull boats into docks in ports, which may often be crowded with other craft, and how to depart from ports. Additional skills that are taught include how to work a ship's communications, electronic, and navigational systems as well as how to log data from ship instruments and handle messages that ships receive.

Certification and Licensing

Watercraft operators must pass a test to retain their US Army Marine Certification every five years. Watercraft operators are licensed to perform special duties like navigation. To get a license, soldiers have to pass a certification test to make sure they have the knowledge and skill for that position. The test is designed to make sure operators know basic information about working on a boat and technical facts about various facets of the jobs they will primarily perform.

Skills and Personality

Watercraft operators have to be comfortable on the water and aboard boats, and they need to be able to endure all kinds of weather at sea. They need to be calm and clearheaded so that they can react quickly in case of emergency. Because organizing and logistics are also part of the watercraft operator's job, a person who is strong in these areas is likely to have success in this job. Being able to work in a tight-knit team as well as act independently when needed are also traits of value to watercraft operators. Knowledge of sailing and navigation is also beneficial, although these skills can be learned during training.

On the official army website, Sergeant First Class Ronald E. Buffkin talks about his job as a watercraft operator aboard the Utility Landing Craft *Kennesaw Mountain*. Buffkin served in Kuwait during the Iraq War. Watercraft operators, he says, have a love and respect for the water. "We have a saying. If it ain't got water under it, we don't want anything to do with it." Because crew members generally work in close quarters, they have to work well together and depend on each other but also be able to take the initiative when needed.

On the Job

Working Conditions

Stormy weather and high seas make the watercraft operator's job a difficult one at times. Life on board the boats can also be challenging, thanks in large part to very limited space. Boat sizes range from smaller Landing Craft Utility boats, which are 115 feet (35 m) long and 34 feet (10.4 m) wide, to the massive Logistics Support Vessel, which is 273 feet (83.2 m) long and 60 feet (18.3 m) wide. Both boats can transport men and supplies, and the Logistics Support Vessel, with 10,500 square feet (975 sq m) of deck space, can carry a huge amount of cargo. Several types of boats serve as landing craft to carry soldiers and supplies, even huge land vehicles like the M1 tank. Although the tanks weigh 60 tons (54.4 metric tons), the army's biggest boats carry twenty-four tanks at one time. The army also has tugboats that can pull US Navy aircraft carriers into new positions in combat areas.

Earnings

The basic pay active duty soldiers receive is based on their rank and length of service. New recruits enter the army as privates, the army's lowest rank. The basic pay for privates is $18,378.00 annually. That base salary goes up steadily, based on rank and length of service. For example, a private first class, the next-highest rank, earns $21,664.80, and that salary increases further every two years he or she serves. Officers earn more than enlisted soldiers, ranging from $34,862.40 for a lieutenant to $52,869.60 for a major.

Salary, however, is just one part of military compensation. Soldiers and their families receive medical and dental care at little or no cost through a military health care plan. Soldiers are also eligible for low-cost group life insurance. Soldiers who live on a military base receive military housing and meals for free. Soldiers who live off a military base receive an allowance to cover their housing and meals. Soldiers also receive allowances for military clothing and official travel. In 2014 the average active duty soldier received a total compensation package of benefits and pay worth $99,000.

Soldiers in combat zones receive $225 per month in hostile fire and imminent danger pay. A variety of salary bonuses is also available for active duty soldiers who serve in foreign countries where the cost of living is high and for reenlisting when their tour of duty is done. Depending on how long they serve, soldiers are also eligible for compensation for a college education when they leave the army. Soldiers get thirty days of vacation annually. Depending on what their missions and training dictate, soldiers are off on weekends and national holidays and get sick days as needed.

Opportunities for Advancement

Any soldier can advance in rank, and even enlisted personnel are able to become officers. Watercraft operators can also advance their careers by learning to do jobs on boats that require more training and expertise. Soldiers stationed on boats work together on some tasks, partly because their crews are not very big. But there are some jobs that require more technical expertise, such as navigating the boat or repairing engines. To be eligible for such jobs, soldiers must pass a test to earn a license that certifies they have the skills to perform that type of work.

What Is the Future Outlook for Watercraft Operators?

In 2016 the army reduced the number of soldiers on active duty in the regular army to 475,000, due to the withdrawal of soldiers from wars in Iraq and Afghanistan. However, it still had 547,007 soldiers in its reserve forces—349,881 in the National Guard and 197,126 in the army reserve. Despite the slight reduction in active duty soldiers, job opportunities for qualified individuals in the army are expected to remain good through 2022, due to continuing military and terrorist threats to the nation's security in various parts of the world.

Since the end of the draft in 1973, the military has met its personnel requirements with volunteers. The army needs to fill entry-level and professional positions as members move up through the ranks, leave the service, or retire. Thus, despite the army drawdown, its recruiting goal for 2016 is 66,500 because of retirements and people leaving the service.

Job opportunities for watercraft operators may increase in the future because of possible problems with Russia and China; the geography of those two nations includes more bodies of water in which army boats could be used than in the mostly landlocked Middle East.

What Are Employment Prospects in the Civilian World?

If a watercraft operator retires or leaves the service, the skills he or she has developed while serving on army boats could be transferred to civilian jobs involving various facets of shipping and handling cargo. Navigators could guide civilian vessels as easily as they could military boats, and techniques for loading and handling cargo would also be the same. In addition, many civilian employers hire veterans to reward them for their service to the country, which will give former watercraft operators an advantage in seeking maritime work.

Unmanned Aircraft Systems Operator

What Does an Unmanned Aircraft Systems Operator Do?

Unmanned aircraft systems operator is an enlisted position. These personnel have become a vital new force in gathering information and for combat. Operators remotely control small aircraft equipped with cameras. These aircraft are known as unmanned aerial vehicles, or more commonly as drones. The drones serve as electronic eyes in the sky to protect soldiers and help battle the enemy in a wide variety of ways. The information that drones reveal about enemy soldiers, such as their location and movement, is vital to "situational awareness," which means understanding what is happening in a combat zone to give soldiers the greatest chance of winning battles. The vital information gathered by unmanned aircraft systems operators includes physical details of possible battle sites such as rivers, hills, and human-made defensive positions.

At a Glance:

Unmanned Aircraft Systems Operator

Minimum Educational Requirements

High school diploma or GED; minimum score of 102 in surveillance and communications on the ASVAB

Personal Qualities

Clear, analytical thinker; detail oriented; good communicator; able to handle multiple tasks at the same time

Working Conditions

Usually in an office setting; sometimes outdoors

Salary Range

Monthly salary depends on pay grade and years of service

Future Job Outlook

Good through 2022

Drone operators also help safeguard soldiers from enemy attack. In a story on the army home page, Staff Sergeant Catalina Avalos says she loves the idea that doing her job well means that "lives were saved downrange." *Downrange* is a military term for the area in which artillery shells land and also means any dangerous area in combat zones. One way in which Avalos saved lives was by spotting people digging holes for improvised explosive devices that could kill and wound soldiers. Avalos was able to send soldiers to deactivate the devices so no one would be harmed.

Added to the difficulty of spotting isolated images that may be important, operators always have to be aware of where they are flying their plane. In a 2013 story on the army home page, Staff Sergeant Nolan Lovett said, "There's a lot of safety concerns involved in operating these vehicles." He said that for safety reasons, operators have to learn to always be aware of the air space the drone is flying in so it will not interfere with other aircraft and cause a collision that could be disastrous.

Operators receive a visual feed on a computer screen of what the plane sees and must constantly monitor it to find anything that will provide new information on enemy soldiers, their location and movement, and what they are doing. At the same time operators are reviewing what the plane sees, they must guide the plane's flight and monitor its mechanical functioning. This is a very technical job because operators work with computers and a variety of software programs to fly planes and perform various missions. Operators launch and fly planes by themselves and guide them in for a landing at the end of each mission. They also must perform continuous checks on the aircraft's electronics and power sources before, during, and after each mission. If anything goes wrong with those systems, they have to know how to fix the problem.

Operators also have to analyze and write reports about the information that they gather. Officers use those reports to plan tactics that will ensure victory and lead to the smallest number of deaths and injuries for their own forces. The reports can also identify possible enemy targets that can be destroyed by artillery or aerial bombing. Some drones are equipped with missiles that operators can fire at targets.

How Do You Become an Unmanned Aircraft Systems Operator?

Education

Students interested in this military occupational specialty should take classes in computer technology, electronics, and physics. Enrolling in a Junior Reserve Officers' Training Corps program will teach students about what military life is like.

Unmanned aircraft systems operators undergo ten weeks of basic combat training and more than twenty-three weeks of advanced individual training. This training occurs in the classroom and in the field with on-the-job instruction. Operators learn how to launch small planes in the air (some need areas as large as a soccer field to get airborne), guide them to designated locations to gather intelligence, and fly them back for a safe landing. Operators are taught how to analyze aerial photographs and video feeds that drones send. They then have to learn how to prepare maps, charts, and reports about that data. Some planes like the Gray Eagle are equipped with weapons such as missiles that can attack enemy positions. Training includes learning the software necessary to guide the plane to its target area and emergency procedures in case the drone's electronic systems fail or function poorly during flight. A training program called VAMPIRE (Visual and Mission Planning Integrated Rehearsal Environment) simulates a flight mission and gives trainees a realistic idea of what it is like to operate a drone. In an Army Strong video, Staff Sergeant Frank Petersen says the job can be difficult: "There's quite a bit of skill involved. . . . A lot of that is information the operator has to know to effectively do his job."

Skills and Personality

Unmanned aircraft systems operators work with extremely sophisticated technology, and because of this they need to be proficient with computer hardware and software. Because they might have to watch enemy troop movements on a computer screen for long periods, they must be patient and able to maintain concentration. When operators see something of interest, they must react quickly and change the plane's flight to get a closer look. When the mission ends, operators have to be able to analyze the information they have gathered and write a report that will be useful in defending against or attacking the enemy. Technical know-how is also important because operators are responsible for launches, landings, monitoring the aircraft's electronics and power sources, and any necessary repairs.

On the Job

Working Conditions

Even though the army is the US military's main land force, part of its mission is accomplished in the air. The aviation branch of the army includes helicopters that perform tasks like transporting soldiers and attacking enemy positions as well as some small fixed-wing planes used mainly for enemy surveillance. The aviation career path in the army includes a variety of jobs such as piloting its helicopters and planes. However, those pilot jobs are limited to officers. There are also many technical positions to keep army aircraft flying, such as electricians, mechanics, and air-traffic controllers, who track army flights and give aircraft landing and takeoff instructions.

One of the newest and most intriguing army aviation jobs is that of the unmanned aircraft systems operator. Army operators perform their jobs in secure army bases stationed near the soldiers they serve. They work long hours sitting in front of computer consoles and monitoring activity on the ground. Staying alert can be a huge challenge. In 2011 Sergeant First Class Kelly C. Boehning was named the army's top unmanned aircraft systems operator. He explains that one of the hardest parts of his job is that it is boring to monitor video feeds for a long time without viewing anything important or interesting: "Basically you look at a field [of activity] for hours and hours and hours and hours, waiting for something to happen. It's not very exciting." But Boehning stresses that an operator has to always remain alert to spot even small details that may be important, like a flash of light from an enemy position that is firing mortar shells. The operator then has a chance to locate the mortar and contact artillery officers to destroy it so it cannot keep firing at his or her own soldiers. Operators sometimes see the destruction through drones they operate. When that happens, Boehning says operators celebrate because "you know you probably saved somebody's life."

Even though operators are far from combat areas, the drones they fly allow them to take an active part in the fighting. Army lieutenant colonel Douglas A. Pryer believes that like other soldiers in combat, they can be wounded psychologically by seeing or even just knowing the destruction and deaths for which they are responsible. In a 2014 newspaper article, Pryer said, "Americans tend to see drones as a means toward an ideal—harming the enemy without being harmed. This ideal is actually impossible to achieve."

Earnings

The basic pay active duty soldiers receive is based on their rank and length of service. New recruits enter the army as privates, the army's lowest rank. The basic pay for privates is $18,378.00 annually. That base salary goes up steadily, based on rank and length of service. For example, a private first class, the next-highest rank, earns $21,664.80, and that salary increases further every two years he or she serves. Officers earn more than enlisted soldiers, ranging from $34,862.40 for a lieutenant to $52,869.60 for a major.

Salary, however, is just one part of military compensation. Soldiers and their families receive medical and dental care at little or no cost through a military health care plan. Soldiers are also eligible for low-cost group life insurance. Soldiers who live on a military base receive military housing and meals for free. Soldiers who live off a military base receive an allowance to cover their housing and meals. Soldiers also receive allowances for military clothing and official travel. In 2014 the average active duty soldier received a total compensation package of benefits and pay worth $99,000.

Soldiers in combat zones receive $225 per month in hostile fire and imminent danger pay. A variety of salary bonuses is also available for active duty soldiers who serve in foreign countries where the cost of living is high and for reenlisting when their tour of duty is done. Depending on how long they serve, soldiers are also eligible for compensation for a college education when they leave the army. Soldiers get thirty days of vacation annually. Depending on what their missions and training dictate, soldiers are off on weekends and national holidays and get sick days as needed.

Opportunities for Advancement

Unmanned aircraft systems operators can advance in rank as they gain more experience and expertise. Demonstrating proficiency on the job and handling increased authority and responsibility can lead to becoming an officer.

What Is the Future Outlook for Unmanned Aircraft Systems Operators?

In 2016 the army reduced the number of soldiers on active duty in the regular army to 475,000, due to the withdrawal of soldiers from wars in Iraq and Afghanistan. However, it still had 547,007 soldiers in its reserve forces—349,881 in the National Guard and 197,126 in the army reserve. Despite the slight reduction in active duty soldiers, job opportunities for qualified individuals in the army are expected to remain good through 2022, due to continuing military and terrorist threats to the nation's security in various parts of the world.

Since the end of the draft in 1973, the military has met its personnel requirements with volunteers. The army needs to fill entry-level and professional positions as members move up through the ranks, leave the service, or retire. Thus, despite the army drawdown, its recruiting goal for 2016 is 66,500 because of retirements and people leaving the service.

The growing use of unmanned aircraft and new technical developments that allow them to do increasingly more important tasks may increase the number of jobs available in the future.

What Are Employment Prospects in the Civilian World?

The use of drones in both the military and civilian life is relatively new. This intriguing new technology is still developing, and it is believed that in the future drones will be used for a wide variety of purposes in civilian life. Amazon, the giant Internet retailer, is considering using drones to deliver packages. Drones can also be used for searching for lost people, monitoring rescue or criminal situations, surveying for construction or environmental projects, and even relaying images for sports or news coverage. Thus, operators should be able to use the skills they have developed in the military to find work in civilian life. And because many employers like to hire veterans to reward them for serving the country, job prospects should be reasonably good for operators.

Signal Officer

Communication is critical to the army's continued success in all of its combat and peacetime missions. The Signal Corps is responsible for army communication systems that transmit and receive voice, data, and other types of information from a variety of sources, including satellites and the Internet. Signal officers are responsible for planning various types of communications for their units. They also oversee soldiers under their command to make sure they properly perform their missions and tasks. These officers need to have working knowledge of the army's communication systems and what to do if those systems are disrupted. Signal officers must also be able to make tactical decisions on how to use those systems most efficiently and to keep them operating at all times, whether they are working in an office on a secure military base or in the field in combat situations when lives may be in danger.

Signal officers are part of the army's computers and technology group. The soldiers under their command include information technology specialists

At a Glance:
Signal Officer

Minimum Educational Requirements
BS degree in electrical or electronics engineering or comparable educational background

Personal Qualities
Physically fit; capable of making decisions quickly and under pressure; able to handle multiple tasks at the same time; disciplined

Certification and Licensing
Secret security clearance

Working Conditions
In an office setting or in the field

Salary Range
Monthly salary depends on pay grade and years of service

Future Job Outlook
Good through 2022

who operate and maintain the army's extensive computer system. Signal officers also oversee specialists in other areas, including those who maintain and operate army radio, microwave, and satellite communication systems. Signal collection analysts intercept, translate, and analyze enemy communications. There are also jobs involving building and fixing various Signal Corps communication systems. Computers and the Internet are a major form of army communications. However, they are vulnerable to attack by the enemy, as are civilian forms of such communication and data storage. In 2015 the army opened its Cyber Center of Excellence at Fort Gordon, Georgia, to train soldiers and civilian Defense Department workers both to launch Internet attacks and defend against such attacks by enemies of the United States. Major General LaWarren Patterson is the commander of the center. In a 2014 story, Patterson promised that "all cyber space operators who [graduate] will report to the operational army ready to stand guard on the digital battlefield of the cyber domain."

Signal officers command soldiers whose job it is to ensure that all the army's communication systems are operating efficiently. They also work to make sure communication systems are secure and safe from enemy attacks, including computer systems that can be invaded by hackers. For example, in an Army Strong video, Captain Justin Miller, who works in information management, explains, "I'm responsible for server management, server configuration—ensuring the network is secure, and we're keepin' people out that don't need to be on the network."

How Do You Become a Signal Officer?

Education

Students interested in this military occupational specialty should take computer technology courses. Since a college degree is required for this position, students are advised to enroll in the Reserve Officers' Training Corps while they are in college. This program provides important preparation for officer training and for military life; it would also help pay for a college education. A bachelor of science degree in electrical or electronics engineering or a similar educational background is required for this highly technical job. This position also requires the person to attain officer rank. Recruits can become officers by graduating from the US Military Academy at West Point, attending the army's Officer Candidate School, or graduating from college in the Reserve Officers' Training Corps. People in certain professional fields, like law, medicine, and the ministry, that require a lot of training can be directly commissioned as officers. Signal officer training includes completion of the Signal Officer Basic Course at Fort Gordon, Georgia. The sixteen-week course teaches candidates how to operate information systems and other tools used in the Signal Corps. Candidates also learn leadership skills, tactics, maintenance, and how Signal Corps systems and tools are used for various tasks. Candidates must also be able to qualify for a secret security clearance, which means their past will be investigated for criminal or possibly anti-American activities.

Skills and Personality

Proficiency with computers and communications technology is essential for the job of signal officer. Candidates for this position have to be able to handle multiple tasks at the same time and be able to think quickly and respond to emergencies, even life-threatening ones in combat. That ability to think quickly and create order out of chaos by directing men they command to do what is necessary is the key to being an officer.

On the Job

Working Conditions

Signaleers, as Signal Corps officers are known, often work in the comfort of an office, but in a war zone they can easily find themselves working in tents, caves, or out in the open. Regardless of the setting, information must continue to flow—both to and from troops. In an Army Strong video, Captain Michael Pope explains, "As a signal officer my primary purpose is to give a field environment the same functionality that you would have in an office building." This can be very challenging. In addition to the threat of enemy fire, Signal Corps personnel in the field often have to struggle with equipment malfunctions brought on by extreme weather or temperatures. However, even under difficult situations in the field, new technology like the satellite transport terminal can keep communications active. In an Army Strong video, Captain Justin Miller explains how easy the piece of equipment is to use: "It's plug and play. [We] can take this to the middle of nowhere in Afghanistan, set it up, and pull a signal. And it's gonna provide data and voice communications for our [soldiers]."

When unexpected things happen—whether their equipment fails or is destroyed or the enemy attacks their position—signal officers have to be able to make quick decisions and give orders to soldiers under their command to cope with the emergency. Signal officers can function in such situations because of the training they have received. The overall expertise and knowledge signal officers have about all Signal Corps communication systems enables them to know how to cope with problems with the equipment. And signal officer training includes how to make tactical decisions during combat and other similar emergencies.

Earnings

The basic pay active duty soldiers receive is based on their rank and length of service. New recruits enter the army as privates, the army's lowest rank. The basic pay for privates is $18,378.00 annually. That base salary goes up steadily, based on rank and length of service. For example, a private first class, the next-highest rank, earns $21,664.80, and that salary increases further every two years he or she serves. Officers earn more than enlisted soldiers, ranging from $34,862.40 for a lieutenant to $52,869.60 for a major.

Salary, however, is just one part of military compensation. Soldiers and their families receive medical and dental care at little or no cost through a military health care plan. Soldiers are also eligible for low-cost group life insurance. Soldiers who live on a military base receive military housing and meals for free. Soldiers who live off a military base receive an allowance to cover their housing and meals. Soldiers also receive allowances for military clothing and official travel. In 2014 the average active duty soldier received a total compensation package of benefits and pay worth $99,000.

Soldiers in combat zones receive $225 per month in hostile fire and imminent danger pay. A variety of salary bonuses is also available for active duty soldiers who serve in foreign countries where the cost of living is high and for reenlisting when their tour of duty is done. Depending on how long they serve, soldiers are also eligible for compensation for a college education when they leave the army. Soldiers get thirty days of vacation annually. Depending on what their missions and training dictate, soldiers are off on weekends and national holidays and get sick days as needed.

Opportunities for Advancement

The lowest officer rank is lieutenant, but as soldiers gain more experience and develop more skills, they can advance in rank all the way to general. Even enlisted soldiers can wind up as high-ranking officers. Emmett Paige Jr. joined the army in 1947 when he dropped out of school at age sixteen. After five years Paige went to the Signal Corps Officer Candidate School. He was commissioned as a lieutenant in 1952 and began a successful career as an officer in which he rose to the rank of lieutenant general before retiring in 1988.

What Is the Future Outlook for Signal Officers?

In 2016 the army reduced the number of soldiers on active duty in the regular army to 475,000, due to the withdrawal of soldiers from wars in Iraq and Afghanistan. However, it still had 547,007 soldiers in its reserve forces—349,881 in the National Guard and 197,126 in the army reserve. Despite the slight reduction in active duty soldiers, job opportunities for qualified individuals in the army are expected to remain good through 2022, due to continuing military and terrorist threats to the nation's security in various parts of the world.

Since the end of the draft in 1973, the military has met its personnel requirements with volunteers. The army needs to fill entry-level and professional positions as members move up through the ranks, leave the service, or retire. Thus, despite the army drawdown, its recruiting goal for 2016 is 66,500 because of retirements and people leaving the service.

The increasing importance of the role communications plays in how the army performs its tasks, including in the new arena of cyber-warfare, is likely to increase the number of positions open for signal officers as well as those in related jobs in the computers and technology career path.

What Are Employment Prospects in the Civilian World?

Modern technology, from the Internet to satellites to mobile phones, has changed the world greatly in the past few decades. Although technological advances have changed the way the army performs its many tasks, they have had an even greater effect on civilian life. Signal officers can expect to qualify for a wide variety of civilian jobs involving communications because of the skills they have developed in the army. Signal officers deal not only with computers and the Internet but radio, telephones, and other forms of electronic communication. And because signal officers command large groups of soldiers, once they leave the service they would be an easy fit for managerial positions in their field in many companies. In addition, many businesses like to hire veterans to reward them for their service.

Military Police

Positions in the military police (MPs) are for enlisted soldiers. MPs are, in effect, equivalent to civilian police officers. They provide security at military bases and enforce military laws and regulations as well as civilian laws such as theft, battery, rape, and murder. They monitor and control vehicle traffic and are trained to respond to emergency situations in which people require assistance, such as a person injured in a car crash or someone who has been physically or sexually assaulted.

MPs also perform a wide variety of tasks in combat zones, including providing security at bases and other less-secure areas and controlling vehicular traffic to make it harder for the enemy to move freely. They collect information by interviewing people, some of them suspected enemies, and conduct raids on homes and people hostile to US forces to eliminate possible threats to fellow soldiers. They are responsible for detaining and sometimes imprisoning enemy soldiers or citizens opposed to US forces.

The basic duty of MPs is to protect the lives of fellow soldiers

At a Glance:
Military Police

Minimum Educational Requirements
High school diploma or GED; minimum score of 91 on the skilled technical portion of the ASVAB

Personal Qualities
Physically fit; able to make decisions and act on them quickly; able to handle stress; good with different types of people

Certification and Licensing
Secret security clearance to read documents classified as confidential

Working Conditions
On secure bases and in combat zones

Salary Range
Monthly salary depends on pay grade and years of service

Future Job Outlook
Good through 2022

both at home and overseas. In an Army Strong video, Staff Sergeant Marcus Brown sums up his job as an MP by saying, "When we're at home, we fight crime. Overseas, we fight the bad guys. We bring law to the lawless all over the world." The latter action occurs in combat zones when MPs help make bases and other areas in combat zones safe from attack. In the same video, Sergeant Ryann Calvaruzo says, "We're here to help people every day and our motto is 'Assist, Protect and Defend.'"

There are many female MPs. Tulsi Gabbard, a member of the US House of Representatives from Hawaii, served as an MP in 2008 in Kuwait, where she helped train the Kuwait National Guard. More women than ever before are serving in positions like MP as the army moves toward integrating women into combat roles. In an article in the *Hill* newspaper, Gabbard said some members of the army lack confidence that female soldiers can perform some jobs. Gabbard was critical of an officer who once declined to use the police platoon she led to provide security for a convoy of trucks. Said Gabbard: "The context for how you decide who goes on a mission should be the best equipped and the most capable. Gender should not be a question in that decision."

The army, like other branches of the military, maintains its own legal and law enforcement system to keep people and property safe. In addition to MPs, this career path includes jobs for firefighters; criminal investigation specialists, who handle felonies involving army property and personnel; and military dog handlers, who work with service dogs for base security and in combat operations. There are also judges who decide cases involving offenses of the Uniform Code of Military Justice, a legal system for all branches of the military. It covers many civilian criminal offenses, like rape and murder, as well as acts by soldiers that harm military order and discipline. When soldiers are found guilty on military charges, they can be sentenced to terms of imprisonment. Another job in the legal and law enforcement field is an internment/resettlement specialist. These specialists work in military correctional facilities in which soldiers convicted of crimes are imprisoned. They also work in military facilities that house servicepeople suspected of being a danger to their fellow soldiers.

How Do You Become a Member of the Military Police?

Education

Students who have an interest in MP jobs should seek out youth programs offered by some police or sheriff's departments. The Teen Police Academy in Fairfax County, Virginia, is one of many such programs offered nationwide. These week-long programs introduce students to the basics of police work, such as patrolling and crime scene investigation. Interested students can also participate in Junior Reserve Officers' Training Corps programs to learn about military life.

Recruits have to take the Armed Services Vocational Aptitude Battery to see whether they are qualified to be an MP. Recruits have twenty weeks of basic combat training and advanced individual training in their field. This instruction in police methods includes time in the classroom and in the field. The training includes learning combat skills all soldiers are taught, as well as how to handle many different firearms. Recruits learn about civilian and military law, including how to determine which of those legal systems should handle a crime or incident to which they are called. There is also classroom and field training in how to investigate crimes and collect evidence, how to control traffic and crowds, and how to arrest and restrain suspects.

Certification and Licensing

MPs handle personal data involving soldiers who are charged with crimes. For this reason, they must receive clearance to read documents classified as confidential. They must also be able to qualify for a secret security clearance, which means their past will be investigated for criminal or possibly anti-American activities.

Skills and Personality

MPs need to be physically fit and emotionally stable to handle dangerous situations involving criminals or enemies. They need to be good with people. Being able to talk with and question strangers and put them at ease is a big plus for someone who wants to work in this kind of job. A desire to help people is also important; MPs are often called on to assist victims of crimes or help with other emergencies. In 2014, for instance, Sergeant Harry Nixon was patrolling a US base in Miesau, Germany, when he saw an older man fall off his bicycle. According to an Army Strong story, Nixon, who is an MP, went to help the civilian, who was a diabetic suffering from low blood sugar. Nixon called an ambulance and was credited by authorities with saving the man's life.

On the Job

Working Conditions

As in any law enforcement job, MPs will often encounter dangerous situations. Even when serving on bases in the United States, the people they have to arrest and the criminal and emergency situations they deal with can place their lives in danger. The level of danger naturally rises when they serve in combat zones. And during the wars in Iraq and Afghanistan, the combat role of MPs became even riskier because their job changed to include searching for improvised explosive devices. MPs manned key intersections and roads to prevent the enemy from carrying explosive devices into cities, where they could do the most damage. Dogs trained to sniff out explosives were a key part of that effort. MPs also provided security on military bases and in urban areas to reduce the threat of such attacks on fellow soldiers and the civilian population. The possibility of explosives detonating while MPs did their job constantly put their lives at risk. MPs also began training the Iraqi police to do the same jobs.

One of the major problems in fighting the Iraq and Afghanistan wars was being able to recognize enemies, because they blended in so well with the general population. The combat mission of MPs expanded to include conducting raids on suspected enemy houses, arresting suspects, and detaining them for questioning.

MPs in both those wars also spent a lot of time patrolling urban areas and interviewing citizens to find out what they knew about possible enemies or their movements. Because MPs worked most of the time outside secure military bases, they were one of the groups of soldiers most heavily involved in combat situations as they continually encountered armed enemies in a variety of situations.

Earnings

The basic pay active duty soldiers receive is based on their rank and length of service. New recruits enter the army as privates, the army's lowest rank. The basic pay for privates is $18,378.00 annually. That base salary goes up steadily, based on rank and length of service. For example, a private first class, the next-highest rank, earns $21,664.80, and that salary increases further every two years he or she serves. Officers earn more than enlisted soldiers, ranging from $34,862.40 for a lieutenant to $52,869.60 for a major.

Salary, however, is just one part of military compensation. Soldiers and their families receive medical and dental care at little or no cost through a military health care plan. Soldiers are also eligible for low-cost group life insurance. Soldiers who live on a military base receive military housing and meals for free. Soldiers who live off a military base receive an allowance to cover their housing and meals. Soldiers also receive allowances for military clothing and official travel. In 2014 the average active duty soldier received a total compensation package of benefits and pay worth $99,000.

Soldiers in combat zones receive $225 per month in hostile fire and imminent danger pay. A variety of salary bonuses is also available for active duty soldiers who serve in foreign countries where the cost of living is high and for reenlisting when their tour of duty is done. Depending on how long they serve, soldiers are also eligible for compensation for a college education when they leave the army. Soldiers get thirty days of vacation annually. Depending on what their missions and training dictate, soldiers are off on weekends and national holidays and get sick days as needed.

Opportunities for Advancement

MPs have opportunities to advance in rank and even become officers by going to Officer Candidate School. They can also receive extra training for more advanced positions like criminal investigations special agent. Like detectives on civilian police forces, these agents investigate felony-level crimes involving army personnel and property.

What Is the Future Outlook for Military Police?

In 2016 the army reduced the number of soldiers on active duty in the regular army to 475,000, due to the withdrawal of soldiers from wars in Iraq and Afghanistan. However, it still had 547,007 soldiers in its reserve forces—349,881 in the National Guard and 197,126 in the army reserve. Despite the slight reduction in active duty soldiers, job opportunities for qualified individuals in the army are expected to remain good through 2022, due to continuing military and terrorist threats to the nation's security in various parts of the world.

Since the end of the draft in 1973, the military has met its personnel requirements with volunteers. The army needs to fill entry-level and professional positions as members move up through the ranks, leave the service, or retire. Thus, despite the army drawdown, its recruiting goal for 2016 is 66,500 because of retirements and people leaving the service.

What Are Employment Prospects in the Civilian World?

The job duties of an MP are similar to that of a police officer in civilian life. The skills MPs learn in the army give them a solid base of experience that makes them strong candidates to be hired for law enforcement jobs on city police departments, county sheriff's departments, and federal agencies like the FBI. In addition, the organization of civilian law enforcement agencies is patterned after the structure of the military in that positions and the duties that officers have in them are based on rank. Law enforcement officials know that army veterans are accustomed to such a structure and know how it works. Veterans are also disciplined in following orders from their superiors as well as having the confidence to act on their own initiative when situations call for independent action.

Human Resources Specialist

Human resources specialist is a position for enlisted soldiers. These specialists deal with soldiers on an individual basis as well as in larger military groups such as a company, division, or battalion. Although the army's basic structure is based on military rank, it functions in some ways like a large civilian corporation; soldiers are treated as employees, and human resources specialists perform tasks similar to their counterparts in civilian businesses.

These specialists work in the army career path of administrative support, a job category for soldiers who meet employee needs for more than 475,000 active duty soldiers as well as men and women in the army reserve and National Guard. Administrative jobs in this category range from clerical positions to supervisory posts like financial manager, an officer who buys services and supplies to keep various army units functioning.

At a Glance:
Human Resources Specialist

Minimum Educational Requirements

High school diploma or GED; minimum score of 90 on the clerical section of the ASVAB

Personal Qualities

Able to work well with different types of people; good listener; patient; organized

Certification and Licensing

Secret security clearance

Working Conditions

Usually in a secure office setting Sometimes in a van or tent outdoors or in a combat zone

Salary Range

Monthly salary depends on pay grade and years of service

Future Job Outlook

Good through 2022

Enlisted personnel working as financial management technicians deal with budgeting and accounting of army expenses. Unit supply specialists, another enlisted job, maintain army equipment and supplies soldiers need to perform their jobs.

The contact human resources specialists have with soldiers begins when they administer the Armed Services Vocational Aptitude Battery (ASVAB), a job aptitude test required of all recruits. Human resources specialists combine test results with information about the education and job experience of incoming recruits to assess their talents and skills. Specialists then use that information to place recruits in various job classifications for which they are suited. After that, specialists supervise or perform a wide variety of clerical and administrative tasks for soldiers for the entire time they are in the army. Human resources specialists help soldiers with their personal finances; they make sure soldiers get paid on time and also help them get insurance for themselves and their families. Specialists also perform job evaluations, promotions, and reassignments for soldiers. Specialists also process requests for leave, maintain personal contact information, and make sure soldiers continue to get mail when they are transferred or working in combat zones.

Human resources specialists manage and allocate personnel throughout the army by assigning them to army locations around the world. This duty involves filling out travel forms and arranging transportation for soldiers to their new posts. Specialists collect data on the job performance of soldiers and evaluate their work to make sure they are doing their jobs correctly and to make sure all units have the personnel they need to perform their missions. As soldiers gain job experience and their length of service increases, specialists are involved in approving promotions of soldiers to higher rank. When soldiers are punished for personal or work problems, specialists take part in the process of reducing their rank, removing them from their jobs, or even expelling them from the army.

Human resources specialists do small tasks like preparing identification tags for soldiers and helping them schedule vacations. Specialists also help soldiers leaving the army for civilian life. The army's Human Resources Command helps former soldiers find civilian jobs. Specialists also make sure retiring soldiers get their retirement pay on time and that all former soldiers receive the benefits to which they are entitled after serving in the army.

The information human resources specialists collect and monitor on individual soldiers is used to make sure they are doing their jobs satisfactorily. Data on soldiers is also used to collectively assess the overall job performance of companies or divisions. In an Army Strong story, Captain Matthew Riggs, who works in human resources, explains, "The most important duty I am responsible for is the monthly unit status report." Riggs says the report accounts for all equipment and personnel, as well as whether they are capable of performing combat or other missions assigned them. And all of those individual reports combine to provide an accurate assessment of the overall ability of the entire army to perform its task of protecting the nation.

How Do You Become a Human Resources Specialist?

Education

Students interested in this army career should make sure they have good written and verbal communication skills. English, history, and social studies classes can help students improve their writing and speaking skills. Courses in computer technology also provide valuable preparation for this job, since most personnel records are computerized. A Junior Reserve Officers' Training Corps program would help prepare students for military life. A score of 90 on the ASVAB's clerical section is required to begin training for the position of human resources specialist. After basic training, there are nine weeks of advanced individual training for this position. Specialists will learn how to type and be introduced to many business practices, such as how to interview people for information and how to fill out the many forms they will deal with daily.

Certification and Licensing

Because specialists access so much personal information on other soldiers while doing their job, they must qualify for a secret clearance classification.

Skills and Personality

Human resources specialists must have good communication skills, both written and oral. Because they deal with sensitive personal information about soldiers, they must be able to adhere to privacy rules. They must also have good organizational skills, since they deal with reams of information on hundreds or thousands of army personnel. A big part of being a human resources specialist is helping soldiers deal with personal matters. For this reason they must also be good listeners. It is important that people in this job have a desire and willingness to help people solve problems.

On the Job

Working Conditions

Human resources specialists usually do their jobs in secure offices and do not experience the rigorous, unpleasant, and often dangerous conditions other soldiers encounter daily in their jobs. The work of such specialists makes life easier for other soldiers because they either help soldiers with or take care of financial and personal issues involving pay, health care, and scheduling time off. In an Army Strong video, Sergeant First Class Natisha Baylor says the best part of being a human resources specialist is doing things that make daily life easier for her fellow soldiers: "I love the fact that I'm making a difference every day. We are the ones that make sure a soldier doesn't have to worry about anything."

Human resources specialists sometimes have to work in close proximity to combat zones and are sometimes exposed to enemy attacks themselves. And the work they do in such situations may be even more vital in combat zones, where other soldiers daily face injury and even death. When soldiers are stationed overseas, human resources specialists make sure soldiers receive mail from home. The army thus works with the US Postal Service to get letters and packages to soldiers in foreign countries, including soldiers serving in combat zones. In an Army Strong blog, Riggs explains why that task is so important: "Without mail [from friends and family] it would be very difficult to keep your spirits up on a deployment [away from home]."

Another important task that human resources specialists do is notifying families when soldiers are wounded or killed. Specialists use personal contact information to inform spouses, parents, and other family members of what happened to the soldier, how injured soldiers are being cared for, and how family members can contact them. Lieutenant Colonel Daniela A. Allen is the top human resources officer for a brigade, a unit that can have as many as four thousand soldiers. In a 2015 Defense Department article, Allen explains that human resources work is much more than keeping track of statistics: "You're not only accountable to the commander, you're also accountable to the American public—to the families. They need to know their loved ones are being taken care of while they do their job."

Earnings

The basic pay active duty soldiers receive is based on their rank and length of service. New recruits enter the army as privates, the army's lowest rank. The basic pay for privates is $18,378.00 annually. That base salary goes up steadily, based on rank and length of service. For example, a private first class, the next-highest rank, earns $21,664.80, and that salary increases further every two years he or she serves. Officers earn more than enlisted soldiers, ranging from $34,862.40 for a lieutenant to $52,869.60 for a major.

Salary, however, is just one part of military compensation. Soldiers and their families receive medical and dental care at little or no cost through a military health care plan. Soldiers are also eligible for low-cost group life insurance. Soldiers who live on a military base receive military housing and meals for free. Soldiers who live off a military base receive an allowance to cover their housing and meals. Soldiers also receive allowances for military clothing and official travel. In 2014 the average active duty soldier received a total compensation package of benefits and pay worth $99,000.

Soldiers in combat zones receive $225 per month in hostile fire and imminent danger pay. A variety of salary bonuses is also available for active duty soldiers who serve in foreign countries where the cost of living is high and for reenlisting when their tour of duty is done. Depending on how long they serve, soldiers are also eligible for compensation for a college education when they leave the army. Soldiers get thirty days of vacation annually. Depending on what their missions and training dictate, soldiers are off on weekends and national holidays and get sick days as needed.

Opportunities for Advancement

Human resources specialists have the same opportunities to advance in rank as soldiers in other jobs. Specialists who perform their jobs very well and have a lot of skill can even become officers by attending Officer Candidate School.

What Is the Future Outlook for Human Resources Specialists?

In 2016 the army reduced the number of soldiers on active duty in the regular army to 475,000, due to the withdrawal of soldiers from wars in Iraq and Afghanistan. However, it still had 547,007 soldiers in its reserve forces—349,881 in the National Guard and 197,126 in the army reserve. Despite the slight reduction in active duty soldiers, job opportunities for qualified individuals in the army are expected to remain good through 2022, due to continuing military and terrorist threats to the nation's security in various parts of the world.

Since the end of the draft in 1973, the military has met its personnel requirements with volunteers. The army needs to fill entry-level and professional positions as members move up through the ranks, leave the service, or retire. Thus, despite the army drawdown, its recruiting goal for 2016 is 66,500 because of retirements and people leaving the service.

What Are Employment Prospects in the Civilian World?

The duties of army human resources specialists are very similar to those of human resources workers in civilian businesses. It would be fairly easy for specialists to make the transition to civilian human resources jobs. Almost every US company of any size has a human resources department with staff members who assist with hiring and firing and help employees obtain health insurance, process worker compensation claims, get mental health assistance, and more. Job prospects for civilian human resources specialists are expected to be favorable in the coming years, according to the Bureau of Labor Statistics. And the fact that many employers like to hire veterans to reward them for serving the country means that job prospects for former specialists are good. In an Army Strong video, Baylor says she is confident that she will be able to "work in a large corporation and get one of the top paying jobs" whenever she decides to leave the army.

Interview with an Infantryman

Juan Garcia joined the army in August 2001 while still in high school in Oxnard, California. Because he was not yet eighteen, his parents had to give their consent for him to join. He began his military career in the infantry and saw combat in Iraq during a tour of duty that began in 2006. Garcia left the army in 2010. He is now a police officer in Milwaukee, Wisconsin.

Q: Why did you join the army?

A: One of the reasons was for the education benefits. My parents were immigrants from Mexico, we didn't have a lot of money, and I knew that [veteran benefits] would help me realize my dream of attending college. But I joined one month before the 9/11 attacks. After that I realized more that [serving in the military] was the honorable, patriotic thing to do. I was able to give something back to my country and I began to love that about being in the army.

Q: Why did you join the infantry?

A: They are the ones who are on the frontlines doing the fighting. I wanted to do that.

Q: How did you train for this career?

A: Infantry training was actually fun. You were constantly training in tactical movements like kicking down doors and how to clear rooms [in dangerous situations] and approach considerations you had to make in entering buildings or going to places [where enemies might be waiting in ambush]. And you were always around weapons; you learned about small weapons and big weapons and about marksmanship and how to shoot. You learned to be part of a six-man team and how to communicate with each other through hand signals.

Q: What was hard about being in the infantry?

A: I hated it at times because it is very physical . . . a lot of working out and running. And you are outside all the time training in all kinds of weather. When it is raining you have trouble staying dry, when it is hot you try to stay cool, and when it is cold you try to stay warm . . . but that's not always possible. And you can never sleep and eat right. Your mentality is that you are always in misery.

Q: What did you like about being in the infantry?

A: The camaraderie. It's hard to explain unless you were in the military. But it's the sense of brotherhood, knowing that you have to take care of that person next to you. Even though we might be miserable, we respected each other and stayed with each other and we would do anything we could for each other. The only people who understand that feeling is someone who has been there.

Q: Can you describe your typical workday?

A: A typical workday [in combat] was waking up and making sure your service weapon is clean and read to use. You had to make sure your mindset was a good one, that you were ready to do anything you could to protect yourself and your fellow soldiers. It was easier otherwise, you were mainly just training . . . but you still had to have that feeling of being ready to do whatever was necessary that day even if it was only training.

Q: What was it like to be in combat?

A: It's not like in the movies or video games; nothing like that. With my experience I call it the *Matrix* effect from the *Matrix* movies [in which martial arts scenes were slowed down so the character could fight.] That's exactly how everything happens, when you have to make that split [-second] decision on whether to pull the trigger and people are firing at you. Everything slows down and you can see and smell things that you never have before. It is the scariest feeling in the world. And it's amazing how your body will react to it without you even knowing because of your training.

Q: What personal qualities are most valuable in this type of work?

A: You have to be determined; you have to be honest about yourself; you have to be professional. The hardest thing is you have to do things right because the smallest things are going to hurt you and everyone around you. And your mind has to be focused on toughness; you have to be tough.

Q: What advice do you have for students who might be interested in this career?

A: My advice is to join the military and join the infantry because it is going to be an experience they are going to enjoy. The camaraderie, the bonds they will develop, and the friends that they will make will change their lives drastically. And by serving, they will develop a whole different level of respect for their country. And by putting on that uniform, you will see how much honor people give to you for doing that, which is a great feeling.

Find Out More

About Careers
http://usmilitary.about.com/od/enlistedjobs/a/enlmos.htm
Details on army military occupational specialties are given on this website that has information, articles, and videos on a wide variety of subjects.

Army Strong Stories
http://armystrongstories.com/soldier-blogs
This site by the Army Marketing and Research Group is dedicated to sharing the meaning of what it means to be "Army Strong" through videos and written posts from soldiers, family members, friends, and supporters.

National Guard
www.nationalguard.com
This site has information on joining the National Guard and what a career in it is like.

Official Homepage of the United States Army
www.army.mil
This site contains stories and features about every aspect of army life, including current news by the Army News Service.

Today's Military
http://todaysmilitary.com
This US Department of Defense site has information about careers in the armed forces.

US Army
www.goarmy.com
This army site has information about the active duty army, National Guard, and army reserves.

US Army Careers & Jobs

www.goarmy.com/careers-and-jobs.html

This section of the US Army site explains in detail all the military occupational specialties available, as well as details about training, working and living conditions, pay, benefits, and other aspects of military life.

Other Jobs in the Army

Air and missile defense crew
 member
Aircraft electrician
Ammunition specialist
Animal care specialist
Army public health nurse
Attack helicopter repairer
Automated logistical specialist
Avionic mechanic
Biomedical equipment specialist
Cargo specialist
Chaplain
Chemical, biological, and
 nuclear specialist
Civil affairs specialist
Combat documentation/
 production specialist
Concrete and asphalt equipment
 operator
Cryptologic linguist
Dental specialist
Explosive ordnance disposal
 specialist
Financial management
 technician

Firefighter
Food service specialist
Geospatial intelligence imagery
 analyst
Interior electrician
Interpreter/translator
Medical laboratory specialist
Military working dog handler
Mortuary affairs specialist
Multimedia illustrator
Musician
Parachute rigger
Paralegal specialist
Pharmacy specialist
Psychological operations
 specialist
Public affairs broadcast specialist
Quarrying specialist
Radiology specialist
Radio operator/maintainer
Shower/laundry and clothing
 repair specialist
Small arms/artillery repairer
Special band musician
Watercraft engineer

Index

Picture Credits

Cover: US Army/Capt. Charlie Emmons

6: Accurate Art, Inc.

12: © David Bathgate/Corbis

24: US Army

32: US Army/Sgt. Michael J. MacLeod

About the Author

Michael V. Uschan has written nearly one hundred books, including *Life of an American Soldier in Iraq*, for which he won the 2005 Council for Wisconsin Writers Juvenile Nonfiction Award. It was the second time he won the award. Uschan began his career as a writer and editor with United Press International, a wire service that provided stories to newspapers, radio, and television. He and his wife, Barbara, reside in the Milwaukee suburb of Franklin, Wisconsin.